trotman

REAL LIFE ISSUES:
BEREAVEMENT

REAL LIFE ISSUES

Real Life Issues are self-help guides offering information and advice on a range of key issues that matter to teenagers. Each book defines the issue, probes the reader's experience of it and offers ways of understanding and coping with it. Written in a lively and accessible style, Real Life Issues aim to demystify the areas that teenagers find hard to talk about, providing honest facts, practical advice, inspirational quotes, positive reassurance, and guidance towards specialist help.

Other titles in the series include:

Real Life Issues: Addictions
Real Life Issues: Bullying
Real Life Issues: Confidence & Self-Esteem
Real Life Issues: Coping with Life
Real Life Issues: Eating Disorders
Real Life Issues: Family Break-ups
Real Life Issues: Money
Real Life Issues: Prejudice
Real Life Issues: Sex & Relationships
Real Life Issues: Stress

REAL LIFE ISSUES:
BEREAVEMENT

Dee Pilgrim

Real Life Issues: Bereavement

This first edition published in 2006 by Trotman and Company Ltd
2 The Green, Richmond, Surrey TW9 1PL

© Trotman and Company Limited 2006

Editorial and Publishing Team
Author Dee Pilgrim
Editorial Mina Patria, Editorial Director; Rachel Lockhart, Commissioning Editor; Catherine Travers, Managing Editor; Ian Turner, Editorial Assistant
Production Ken Ruskin, Head of Manufacturing and Logistics; James Rudge, Production Artworker
Sales and Marketing Suzanne Johnson, Marketing Manager
Advertising Tom Lee, Commercial Director

Designed by XAB

British Library Cataloguing in Publication Data
A catalogue record for this book is available from the British Library

ISBN 1 84455 099 0

Typeset by Photoprint, Torquay
Printed and bound in Great Britain by Cromwell Press, Trowbridge, Wiltshire

CONTENTS:

> 'There is life after bereavement and you will know when you feel able and ready to start living it.'

REAL LIFE ISSUES:
Bereavement

ABOUT THE AUTHOR

Dee Pilgrim trained to be a journalist at the London College of Printing. After graduation she worked for a variety of music and women's titles including *Sounds*, *Company*, *Cosmopolitan*, *Ms London*, *New Woman* and *Girl About Town*. After going freelance she concentrated on celebrity interviews and film, theatre, music and restaurant reviews. She is currently the Film Editor for *NOW* magazine and is active within the Critics' Circle, helping to organise its annual film awards event. She has written a number of titles for Trotman, including five Real Life Guides, and also a book on money for the Real Life Issues series.

REAL LIFE ISSUES:
Bereavement

ACKNOWLEDGEMENTS

I owe a huge debt of gratitude to counsellor Nicky Martin, who not only had the initial idea for a book on bereavement specifically for teenagers, but also helped with many insights gained during the course of her work with the bereaved. I would also like to thank crisis counsellor B M Shaughnessy, whose experiences working with young people in London and in Canada were invaluable when I came to write about bereavement as a result of suicide or an act of violence. Finally, thank you to the organisations listed in Chapter 10 of this book for pointing me in the right direction.

INTRODUCTION:
What this book is all about

'Oh, if you felt the pain I feel!
But oh, whoever felt as I!'
Written by the Greek poet Sappho, around 630 BC.
Translated by Walter Landor.

Nothing and no one can ever really prepare us for the loss of someone we love. Be they a grandparent, parent, brother, sister, friend or even a beloved pet, as the poet Sappho eloquently says, the pain is so devastating and so raw that you truly believe no one could ever have felt as you feel. In one way this is true, because everyone's experience of bereavement is unique and personal to them. However, it is also an experience we will all face at some time in our lives, for death is the one thing we can rely on. It is the natural ending to the circle of life, the final farewell to this world and everything in it we hold dear.

In the normal scheme of things, death comes at the end of an active and fulfilling life, and some teenagers are lucky enough to go through their entire childhoods without ever losing a loved one. But death is no respecter of age and many young people will find themselves having to deal with the grief of bereavement early in life. According to the Office for National Statistics, in the UK 53 children are bereaved of a parent every day – that's more than one every half hour, adding up to almost 20,000 every year. The figure for those who suffer the loss of a grandparent, friend or sibling far exceeds this. Apparently, 13% of children aged between 5 and 15 have experienced the death of a grandparent. That is equivalent to 1,105,000 children in the UK.

> 'Grieving ... is the mind and body's way of healing itself after a catastrophic shock to the system.'

For those who are left behind the loss can be devastating, particularly for teenagers because it goes against everything they believe in. 'They believe they are invincible, that they are going to live forever,' says social worker and bereavement counsellor Nicky Martin. 'Everything about teenage years is about the future and what they will be going on to do later in life, so when someone close to them dies it is at odds with the way teenagers feel.'

LETTING IT ALL OUT

Coming to terms with bereavement is never easy, especially in a society where we rarely talk about death, let alone celebrate it. Death and the fear of dying is one of our remaining unspoken taboos. It's one of those subjects we tend to shy away from and so when we are forced to deal with it – when someone we love dies, or when a friend is bereaved – we are at a loss as to what to do and what to say in order to 'make it better'. Because of this, many people shut their grief away and put on a brave face. However, experts believe that if you do not go through the natural grieving process you could be storing up problems, both emotional and physical, for yourself in the future. Apparently, thoughts of suicide occur in up to 54% of survivors after a death, regardless of whether they grieve or not, and may continue for up to six months. Depressive illness occurs in 17–27% of survivors during the first year after a death. That's why it is so important to give yourself permission to grieve, to let yourself mourn – it is the mind and body's way of healing itself after a catastrophic shock to the system.

BEING PREPARED

As stated earlier, everyone grieves in their own way and at their own speed – there is no right way or wrong way. If you come from a religious background there may be rites and ceremonies you need to perform in order to honour the dead, yet you may still find yourself emotionally 'in mourning' even when the customary mourning period or rituals are over. Alternatively, you may have physical symptoms that make you feel like a freak. Questions such as 'Why can't I stop crying?', 'Why do I keep dreaming about her?' or 'Why does that song keep going round and round my head?' may plague your waking hours until you believe you're going mad. The truth is, you're not: all of these symptoms are normal. You may experience some of them or none at all. You may go through all the stages of grief or skip some of them completely. You may get over your grief in six months or it may take longer. There are no set rules and no easy remedies. However,

'There is life after death for those of us who are left behind – the key is to find a way through the agony that is bereavement to the life that is the future.'

knowing what to expect and realising that other people have been through what you are experiencing may help you cope better with the whole process.

That is why this book exists – to give you the pointers you need to help you deal with an emotional pain that can be all-consuming. It will not magically take away the heartache you are suffering, but it will:

- Explain the different stages and symptoms of bereavement
- Tell you where and who you can turn to for help
- Give you some tips on things you can do to help yourself.

'I think the young people who can say "I need help" are already doing their bereavement work,' says crisis counsellor B M Shaughnessy. 'However, this book could be a way for people who can't ask someone directly for help to get it.'

If you are a friend of someone who has recently been bereaved you may desperately want to do something for them, but not know what to say or where to start. This book will tell you why they may be acting in the way they are, and Chapter 5 will give you positive advice on what you can do to help them through this extremely difficult and distressing time.

Death is never easy; as living, breathing, constantly evolving beings, we find its finality not only shocking but also somehow obscene. But there is life after death for those of us who are left behind – the key is to find a way through the agony that is bereavement to the life that is the future.

CHAPTER ONE:

MANY WAYS TO SAY GOODBYE
Tradition and grieving

The need to say goodbye to those who have died – to mourn their loss and to symbolically remember their life – cuts across all levels of society and all religious beliefs. It seems to be a natural, human response to the deaths of those we love. Like many other landmark dates in our lives – our passage into adulthood, marriage, the birth of a child – we feel the need to celebrate our deaths by some form of ceremony that acts as a memorial. As these acts or rites tend to involve not only family members but also friends and associates of the dead person, they can often work as a form of group therapy, giving added comfort and support to those who attend.

'The need to say goodbye to those who have died – to mourn their loss and to symbolically remember their life – cuts across all levels of society and all religious beliefs.'

DIFFERENT TIMES

The way we choose to symbolically mark the death of someone close is dependent on many things, including cultural traditions, where we live, and how affluent we are. In ancient Egypt, for instance, the immensely wealthy pharaohs commissioned vast tombs and pyramids to mark their passing, and because they believed in a life after death they were often buried with items of furniture, flagons of wine and containers of food to sustain them in the afterlife.

Here in Britain, the Victorians wore special black clothing (widows' weeds) as a mark of respect for the dead and held elaborate funeral rites which, as counsellor B M Shaughnessy explains, have enormous symbolic importance as transitional acts. 'They help the bereaved get through this difficult time,' she explains, 'so they are very important in the symbolic recovery of the person (who has been bereaved).'

Apparently, the Victorians were also fond of keeping locks of the departed's hair to be woven into lockets or other trinkets so they could feel they were keeping a piece of them close. Counsellor Nicky Martin says, 'death may end life but not the relationship you have with this person and so it is OK to hold on to the memory.' This is still true today and many people 'hold on' to something of the dead person's that has special meaning for them – a favourite T-shirt, a piece of jewellery, a much loved photograph or postcard – in order to keep them close (this is discussed in more depth in Chapter 6: How can I help myself?).

DIFFERENT PLACES

Inhumation, or interment in the ground (burial), has traditionally been the practice in very hot climates where bodies must be buried as quickly as possible before they start to break down. In areas close to large bodies of water (such as in India, by the banks of the River

Ganges) the body would be set adrift on the water, the current or tide symbolically taking it away from the world of the living. In areas where wood or other sources of fuel are abundant the body may be cremated on a funeral pyre. Traditionally in Tibet, the method of burial would depend on your social standing and thus how much you could afford to pay for your funeral. The lower classes would place bodies in water; the middle classes would be buried; and the upper classes, who could afford to buy large amounts of precious wood, would be cremated.

DIFFERENT BELIEFS

Religion plays an even greater part in funeral arrangements than where you happen to live or how rich you are:

- Traditional Christian burials may involve a funeral service with readings from scripture and eulogies (tributes) read out by family or friends, followed by a 'wake' or meeting where everyone eats, drinks and commemorates the dead person's life.
- Hindus are cremated, and the mourning period lasts for 13 days. There is a special ceremony for those Hindus who die outside of India: their bodies are cremated and, within a year after the death, members of the family take the remains back to India to be ceremonially thrown into the Ganges.
- In the Jewish faith, cremation is not permitted and the official mourning period of seven days is known as 'shiva', with the immediate family wearing black mourning dress for up to 11 months on the death of a child or parent.
- Muslims bury their dead without a casket, with their heads pointed towards Mecca. Fellow mourners are expected to comfort the deceased's family and to urge them to accept the death as Allah's will, so they can quickly return to their normal routines.

■ In the Sikh religion the mourning period lasts between two and five weeks and the body is cremated after being specially washed and dressed by members of the family.

However, as society becomes increasingly secular (non-religious), the ways people choose to say goodbye become less bound by tradition and formula. Ashes from cremations are often sprinkled on a spot that was the dead person's favourite (for instance, in a garden). They can even be scattered from the back of a boat into the sea. You can have a 'green' burial, where the body is placed in a cardboard (therefore fully recyclable) or birch basket coffin and laid to rest in woodland. And now those who want to go out with a bang can be cremated and have their ashes placed in a firework rocket to be launched in a stunning display (the writer Hunter S Thompson's last wish was to have his remains fired out of a cannon – a wish that was duly honoured when actor Johnny Depp paid for the cannon).

CLOSURE AND ACCEPTANCE

Whichever way a person's death is marked, the actual rite, or 'symbolic action' as B M Shaughnessy describes it, is very important, because it denotes a form of closure for those who are grieving. Many bereaved people describe how they don't really believe or acknowledge the death until they see the coffin disappear behind the curtain at the crematorium or as it is lowered into the ground at a burial. It is only then that the finality of the death can be accepted and the mourning process put into action.

Until recently it was thought that children and young people should not attend funerals because it would be too upsetting for them. In reality, it was often the case that adults didn't want children attending because the adults themselves would become too upset. But young people need to be a part of these 'symbolic actions' as much as adults, in order to show their own respect for the person who has died and to share their own memories and emotions, which are just as valid as those of people older than them. If you are not even asked if you want to attend the funeral, you may feel that your own needs and wishes are being disregarded. However, you should never feel obliged to go if you don't want to; if you don't feel up to it, you can find other ways to mark a transitional act and to say goodbye (see Chapter 6, page 50 for some ideas).

'Attending the funeral or marking some form of transitional act can be one of the first steps on your own road to recovery.'

If you are the friend of someone who has been bereaved, then sharing in some form of funeral rite will not only demonstrate your support for that person, but may also prove personally helpful. For example, after the London bombings of 2005 many people who had become involved, from survivors to members of the emergency services, found sharing memorial services with the bereaved tremendously comforting. If you have been bereaved yourself, attending the funeral or marking some form of transitional act can be one of the first steps on your own road to recovery as you pass through your grief and despair into acceptance.

PHASES OF FEELING
The physical and emotional impact of grief and what you can expect to feel

'No two people mourn in the same way or feel the same things.'

The introduction to this book explained that, although loss through death is something we must all face at some time in our lives, our own experiences of bereavement are unique to us. No two people mourn in the same way or feel the same things. However, there are certain recognised stages or phases to the grieving process.

STAGES OF GRIEF

Psychiatrist Elizabeth Kubler-Ross wrote a number of renowned books on bereavement and she defined five stages of grief that all overlap with each other. One bereaved person might go through all the stages in the clockwise sequence given in the diagram below, but another may miss some stages altogether or experience them in a different sequence.

Phases of feeling

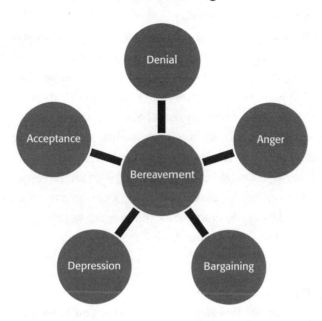

The emotions a bereaved person feels and their intensity will very much depend on how close they were to the person who has died, the circumstances of the death (see Chapter 3 for more on this) and the strength of the support system around them. It's important to emphasise that there is no right or wrong way of experiencing these emotions: not everyone will go through all the stages shown in the diagram, but that doesn't make their grief any less painful or their loss any less traumatic. However, if you have been bereaved and do find yourself experiencing feelings you recognise from the diagram, you can take comfort in knowing they are all totally normal responses – you shouldn't feel guilty for feeling them, as they are part of the natural process of healing. Each stage is outlined in a little more detail under the headings below.

Denial
'This isn't happening to me.'

You must remember that after a loss – even if, as in the case of terminal illness, you had prepared for it – you go into a state of shock. This can manifest itself in the physical symptoms described later in this chapter, but from a psychological point of view you seem to shut down. There is a numbness and a disbelief; you simply cannot accept this is happening to you. It's normal to hear bereaved people say things like 'but he can't be gone', or 'it's not true'. Very sadly, it is – it's just that some part of you can't yet accept the death as reality. You tell yourself it has all been a big mistake and your loved one will walk through the door at any moment, or you may not want to go to bed and sleep for fear you will miss them if they return.

Anger
'How dare you let this happen? How dare you leave me?'

Anger after death can be ferocious in its intensity – you may be:

■ Raging at the person who has died
■ Mad at the medical profession (especially if the death has occurred after an illness)
■ Angry with other members of your family (for not preventing the death)
■ Angry with yourself (because you could not stop this person from leaving you).

This stage of grieving can be very scary because anger is such a strong emotion: you may feel you are out of control. But once again, remember that it's OK to be angry and it's totally normal. In Chapter 6 of this book you will find techniques to help you cope with and disperse your anger without hurting anyone else or yourself.

Bargaining
'If you come back, I promise I'll behave better.'
The weird thing about this stage is that, although you *know* the deceased person isn't going to magically get up and walk again, there's a space in your mind that says they will – but only if you put in a plea bargain. This can be anything from 'if I could just apologise for that nasty thing I said then they wouldn't have to be dead' to 'if I had one more chance, I wouldn't muck it up this time'. However, as the days pass and the person doesn't reappear you will have to acknowledge that, although not forgotten, the person you loved so much is gone and is not coming back. This is when you may be struck by one of the most difficult stages of the grieving process.

Depression
'I'll always feel this lonely. I'll never be happy again.'
The mix of loneliness, hopelessness and despair that is known as 'circumstantial depression' (ie depression brought on by the circumstance of your loss, rather than clinical depression) can be extremely debilitating. You won't want to get out of bed in the mornings – why bother? You may lose interest in food or in your appearance – who is going to care? You may find the smallest thing makes you cry and once you start to weep you simply cannot stop. It may seem as if there is a black cloud sitting over you and, whichever way you turn and whatever you do, you cannot escape from this terrible, appalling sadness. It's at this stage some people may even contemplate suicide and, in this case, even if you don't recognise it yourself, you need professional help (for more information, see Chapter 4).

Depression can be so overwhelming you may decide to turn your back on it and pretend it isn't there, but there is really only one way to get through this pain, and that is to give in to it. It may take you weeks, months or even years to get over and you may find it recedes only to come back more strongly before ebbing away again. So – cry if you want to, let your friends and family know if you are going through a particularly bad phase but, most importantly, allow yourself to feel. There is no shame in admitting you have lost a very important person in your life.

Acceptance

'I'll never forget you, but it's time to get on with my life.'

You will know when you are finally coming to terms with your grief: it's when you accept that the person you love so much is not coming back but thinking about them doesn't send a dagger through your heart – in fact you can think back to good times and find yourself smiling. Acceptance does not mean forgetting, it means embracing your memories. In fact, bereavement counsellors now talk of 'continuing bonds'. 'You hold on to the memory of the person because although the life may have ended with the death, the relationship you have with the dead person does not end, it continues,' explains Nicky Martin. You may still have bad days when you feel you can't cope but you no longer feel the all-encompassing emotions that have rocked you through your mourning. You may still cry but at last there is a chink of blue sky where before there was just blackness, and you find you actually can envisage a future for yourself.

> *'Acceptance does not mean forgetting, it means embracing your memories.'*

Many bereaved people find that the worst days after this are memorable dates such as birthdays (yours or that of the deceased). 'One of the biggest fears those recovering from bereavement have is major dates during the year,' says Nicky. 'The first Christmas after the bereavement may be extremely distressing and also the first anniversary of the death. If you've lost a parent then such milestones as passing your exams or your driving test can set you back and if you've lost a friend such things as going on to university or college while knowing they never will can bring the grief flooding back.' If you think certain dates are going to distress you, Chapter 6 will suggest some positive things you can do to lessen that distress.

Guilt

During your grieving you may also find yourself feeling guilty because you couldn't stop your loved one from dying, or because you don't think you are grieving as much as you should be or as much as the other people around you are. You can experience guilt at any stage of grieving and if you have lost someone through suicide it can be especially troubling. We will talk about suicide in more depth in the next chapter.

PHYSICAL SYMPTOMS

At the very beginning of this book there is a quote from the ancient Greek poet Sappho, as she explains how overwhelming her grief is. In another part of her poem she describes her physical symptoms – her fingers are aching and her lips are dry. Physical manifestations of grief are not uncommon and, as with the emotional stages you pass through, you may experience a range of them, have just one symptom, or have none at all. Some may begin straight after the death occurs while others can come on weeks later. Some symptoms can be mild while others can be alarmingly intense. Whatever physical symptoms you experience, it is important to acknowledge them and to monitor them. If they persist, speak to someone about them and, if necessary, do visit your doctor. The diagram below shows some physical symptoms you might experience:

Physical symptoms

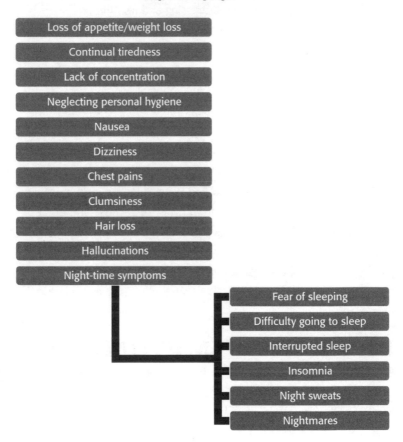

Loss of appetite/weight loss

Continual tiredness

Lack of concentration

Neglecting personal hygiene

Nausea

Dizziness

Chest pains

Clumsiness

Hair loss

Hallucinations

Night-time symptoms

Fear of sleeping

Difficulty going to sleep

Interrupted sleep

Insomnia

Night sweats

Nightmares

Loss of appetite/weight loss

This is one of the most common ways grief manifests itself physically.
Food simply loses all relevance; some people say it actually becomes
tasteless. But bereavement is a terrible shock to your whole system
and so you must take care of yourself. Do try to eat healthy, nourishing
foods. If you feel you can't face three proper meals a day then eat little
and often – a bowl of comforting soup or some fruit rather than a bag
of chips or sweets. Also, sitting down communally to eat with your

family rather than taking your meals alone will give you the opportunity to talk things through with them and to grieve with them.

Tiredness

Grief is exhausting and you may find yourself continually fatigued. Don't feel guilty when you find you have no energy to do things outside of grieving – instead be gentle with yourself. Take things slowly and don't expect to be back to normal in a few days. One mistake many bereaved people make is to throw themselves into a flurry of activity immediately after the death as avoidance – thinking 'if I lose myself in this I won't have to think about my pain'. This can lead to exhaustion and, in addition, it will stop you addressing your grief. Embarking on new projects or hobbies is best left until you are feeling slightly better.

Lack of concentration

Lack of concentration can be a real problem for bereaved children. 'It can seriously affect pupils' progress at school,' explains Nicky Martin. 'However, if they can find someone in school they can really talk to (such as a teacher they really identify with) and let them know things aren't so good then this is a problem that can be addressed.' Don't expect the school to make a big fuss of you – but, once you have told someone in school about your situation, you should find you are given more space while you get back on top of things.

Neglecting personal hygiene

When your whole world is being consumed by sadness, doing things like washing your hair, taking showers or changing your clothes may not even register on your consciousness. However, neglecting yourself is not going to bring your loved one back. Cleanliness is an important issue, not only because warm baths and showers can calm and relax you, but also because they are good for your self-esteem. Many bereaved people feel bad about themselves ('I was a useless daughter/son/friend') and, as mentioned above, may even feel guilty about the death. This can give your self-esteem a real knock, and neglecting personal hygiene and appearance will only make the situation worse. Knowing you look clean and presentable will help you to feel better about yourself, so try to get into a routine where you have a shower or bath every night before going to bed. This can also help you get a better night's sleep, especially if you use products containing calming aromatherapy oils such as lavender and camomile (see the 'Night-time symptoms' section below).

> **For a closer look at self-esteem,**
> **see *Real Life Issues: Confidence & Self-Esteem***

Nausea

Feeling sick to your stomach is a classic sign of stress, as are tummy upsets, and the mourning period can be a very stressful time. This is another reason why it is important to make sure you eat properly. Small, regular meals can help keep nausea at bay while many people say that eating ginger lessens symptoms (ginger being a traditional remedy for travel sickness). However, if the symptoms persist, you should see a doctor.

Dizziness

When you are suffering from mental stress your brain can start to do weird things. No, you are not going mad – dizziness, disorientation and even panic attacks don't mean you have some terrible illness. Remember, these are just symptoms brought on by the turmoil of emotions you are experiencing. Do tell someone about them, though, so they can sit with you and help keep you calm while the dizzy spell or attack passes. Some people find a natural remedy like the flower-based Bach Rescue Remedy can help. If symptoms persist, you must see a doctor to be checked out.

Chest pains

Chest pains can be very scary because it may feel like you are having a heart attack. Many of the teenagers Nicky Martin counsels describe experiencing an actual feeling of physical yearning similar to really bad heartburn. Each breath you take in is an effort and hurts, and it also feels as though your chest is constricted. Once again, it is important to let someone know how you are feeling physically so that they can help keep you calm when you experience the pains – panicking will upset your breathing patterns and make your symptoms worse. Relaxation techniques such as meditation, visualisation and breathing exercises can really help and several of these are described in Chapter 6.

Clumsiness

When your brain is preoccupied by something, as it is during the grieving period, it is very easy to 'forget' yourself. You become less self-aware and, in B M Shaughnessy's experience, this is when accidents can happen. 'Bereaved young people don't harm themselves deliberately,' she explains, 'but they become terribly clumsy. They fall, they cut themselves, partly because their minds have become disassociated – they're not with them – and they need to recollect themselves.' If you recognise this in yourself, you need to take extra care, or get other people to do things for you if you are in danger of harming yourself. If you are a friend of someone who is bereaved and notice this behaviour, then make them aware of it as tactfully as you can, and take extra care to monitor their movements.

Hair loss

Alopecia (hair loss) has recently been in the news after TV presenter Gail Porter lost all her hair through stress. She has been brave enough to bring attention to a condition that isn't often talked about. It's rare for bereaved teenagers to suffer from it – but if you do experience an unusual amount of hair shedding (finding handfuls of hair on your pillow in the morning, or losing large amounts as you brush your hair) you must go to your doctor.

> **For a closer look at the issues connected with stress, see _Real Life Issues: Stress_**

Hallucinations

'A week after my grandmother died, my mother sat bolt upright in bed convinced she could hear her mum calling out her name.' Some people not only suffer from such auditory hallucinations but they also believe they see the dead person in the street or just out of the corner of their eye. This can be very distressing, but it is understandable – you miss this person so much it's almost as if your mind conjures up a hologram of them for you. As you pass through the grieving process so you will gradually find you 'let go' of the dead person – they no longer occupy your every waking thought – and the hallucinations should gradually diminish accordingly.

Night-time symptoms

'You need to remember that even when you are sleeping you are still grieving,' says Nicky Martin. That's why so many bereaved people find their sleeping patterns become disrupted after the death of someone close to them. However, there are strategies you can use and things you can do to keep that disruption to a minimum. The paragraphs below suggest methods of dealing with the various night-time symptoms you may experience.

FEAR OF SLEEPING

The night can be a very lonely, dark place, and one that you may find frightening. Some people worry that if they allow themselves to sleep they, like their loved one, might never wake up. Others are afraid of what they might encounter in their dreams – ghosts, spectres, or maybe images from the past they don't want to be reminded of. You might find having someone else sleeping in the room with you helps – someone you can talk to in bed before you nod off. It may sound childish but leaving the bedroom door open or having a night light in the room can also be reassuring.

DIFFICULTY GOING TO SLEEP

Even if you are not afraid to sleep you may find yourself all tucked up in bed but unable to nod off – however many sheep you count. Once again, a relaxing bath or shower with lavender or camomile oil can help, as can meditation techniques. You may find soothing music makes you drift off, or tapes of ambient sounds such as birdsong or waves lapping against the shore. Reading a chapter of a favourite book or even writing that day's entry into your diary can act as markers for your brain to 'switch off'. You could also try going to bed either half an hour earlier or later than normal to see if this suits your body clock better. Finally, a warming milky drink may just do the trick.

'The night can be a very lonely, dark place.'

INTERRUPTED SLEEP

Once you've finally slipped into sleep, there's no guarantee you will stay that way until morning. Many bereaved people find themselves waking repeatedly during the night. Although short bouts of sleep are better than no sleep at all, they are not ideal. Again, try the trick of altering the time you go to bed to see if that helps. When you do wake during the night, visit the bathroom or get yourself a glass of water before trying to go back to sleep.

INSOMNIA

Not sleeping at all will soon wear you down emotionally and physically. Lying in bed with your eyes wide open, the clock ticking away and no one to talk to can be agony. If you've tried all of the above techniques and nothing is working, there are herbal sleeping remedies available from chemists and health food shops. (Make sure you talk to the pharmacist to check the medication is suitable for you, and always read the label and advice leaflet.) Alternatively, go to your doctor, who may be able to prescribe something to help you through this difficult time.

NIGHT SWEATS

Waking in a pool of sweat can be quite scary because you immediately assume there's something really wrong with you – but night sweats are just a symptom of the stress you are under. Try to make sure your room is well ventilated and your bedding is warm enough but isn't going to make you overheat. Also, make sure your nightclothes are light and loose, preferably made from natural fabrics that allow your skin to breathe. If you wake feeling you are overheating then push the bedclothes back until you cool down again and have a glass of water ready by the side of the bed. If night sweats persist you should visit your doctor.

NIGHTMARES

For some, the nightmare of bereavement doesn't stop when they go to sleep – their dreams are full of unimaginable dread and fear. As Nicky Martin says, you may be sleeping but you are still grieving and the fears you have in waking life – about what the future holds, how you will manage and whether you are ever going to feel 'normal' again – can easily cross over into your dreams. Again, having someone sleeping in the same room as you can help, as can leaving the door open so you can call out to others in the house if you wake up. You could also try keeping a 'dream diary' by the side of the bed in which you jot down your nightmares and then describe what they mean to you. If you are having counselling, discussing nightmares with your counsellor can be really useful as they can help you put them into context. You should never be afraid that admitting you are having nightmares might make people think you are a baby – the fear they instil is real and is not good for you, and you may find talking to someone about them actually makes you feel better.

CHAPTER THREE:

DIFFERENT TYPES OF LOSS
Bereavements you can prepare for and those that are unexpected

'Bereavement is like a secret club. Until somebody dies, you don't know it exists – but when they do, then you join the club.'

David, 15

At some stage in our lives, we must all join the 'secret' bereavement club. Some of us may join while we are still young, others not until we are mature adults. Some become members via the death of a work colleague or distant relative, while others may lose a parent or sibling. The entry point may be through a terminal illness, old age, suicide or a tragic accident. It doesn't matter if the loss is anticipated or not, or if the person who dies is old or young, no loss is easy to bear. All bereavement hurts and how you deal with it will be unique to you. This chapter explores the different types of loss you may experience and the different feelings that loss might evoke.

DIVORCE

Although no one dies in a divorce, it can certainly feel that way. If two people you love break up you can feel caught in the middle, not wanting to show favouritism for either. You may feel guilty ('Was it my fault they split?') and you may feel very fearful ('Where will I live? Will I have to change schools?'). One of the biggest worries is whether you will see the parent you no longer live with regularly.

All this uncertainty can really take its toll on you, as it did to Sally's teenage son Peter when she split with his dad. Normally a 'straight A' student, Peter's grades and his behaviour at school deteriorated dramatically after the split, so much so that Sally was sent a letter. It was only at this stage, when she contacted Peter's teacher, that she discovered he had told no one about what he was going through. Once the school was aware of the situation, it took steps to help Peter through this difficult time and his grades and behaviour began to improve. You may feel embarrassed or ashamed if your parents decide to divorce, but keeping silent will not help you to cope – talking it over with someone will. Remember that divorce is nothing to be ashamed of; it happens to lots of families.

> **For a closer look at this issue,**
> **see *Real Life Issues: Family Break-ups***

LOSS OF A PET

Losing their much-loved guinea pig, hamster, rabbit or cat is often the first experience of death and bereavement a young person will have. Apparently, the majority of pet-owning families in the UK have children, with less than 9% of dogs and 14% of cats living in a childless household. In fact, looking after pets is a great thing for young people to do as it develops their social skills and also gives them a sense of responsibility for another living thing. A pet may be a young person's best friend and confidant, especially if the family has had a dog from puppyhood or a cat from being a kitten, and so when that pet dies the loss can be just as devastating as losing a human friend or relative. Some people may say 'but it's just a stupid cat' – but they didn't know it and they are not grieving for it. You are, and you should grieve for as long and as deeply as you like. All the advice given in this book about mourning for a loved one is just as relevant for a pet as for a person.

LOSS OF A GRANDPARENT

Many young people find it easier to talk to a grandmother or grandfather about their problems than to their parents – it's as if the generation gap skips a full generation – so when grandma or grandpa dies they lose the person they confided in. Grandparents may also fulfil the role of childminder or babysitter and so, having been very close, their loss is all the more keenly felt. Even if a grandparent has been unwell for some time and their death is anticipated, when they do actually die it can still be a shock to the system – so you need someone to talk to about it, especially if your parents are finding it difficult to cope with their own loss.

LOSS OF A PARENT

'One of the worries children have when they lose a parent is that they feel different – their friends don't understand what they are going through and so they feel isolated if they've lost a parent and their friends still have both,' explains counsellor Nicky Martin. 'They also worry about the finances of the household changing. However, the biggest fear of all if they have lost one parent is that the other parent will die.' Teenagers in particular feel the loss of a parent keenly, especially those who have younger brothers or sisters, because they feel very responsible if the other members of the family are coping badly. It's as though they feel they must take over the role of mum or dad even when they are in no emotional state to do so. There is a frantic need to 'hold the family together' and this perceived responsibility can be so stressful that it breeds resentment over the death. All the teenager really wants to do is to return to normal, but things will never be the same again and the grieving does not stop until they can accept this and the new circumstances of their life.

LOSS OF A SIBLING (BROTHER/SISTER)

There can also be resentment when a young person loses their only brother or sister, as Nicky Martin explains: 'If they are left as an only child they can feel huge responsibility to now be the "perfect" child for their parents and they may resent that.' If their sibling was their best friend and confidant, they may feel extremely isolated and lonely as well. This feeling will be even stronger if they shared a room with the sibling and must now sleep alone. If more than one brother or sister survives they may feel guilty if they seem to be getting over the death at different rates. 'If you are still grieving while your siblings have got over it you may think there is something wrong with you,' says Nicky. In addition you may feel guilty that you can't make the pain go away for your parents. In fact, on the death of a child, parents can sometimes get so lost in their own grief they unwittingly neglect the needs of their other children and this is where outside help, in the form of counselling or a bereavement group, can be very beneficial.

LOSS OF A FRIEND

When you are young, the last thing that ever enters your mind is that a friend will die before you. It can be a real shock, says Nicky Martin: 'You may have been planning things together and now that friend is gone. How are you meant to go back to school with the friend not

there any more?' The loss of a friend can be all-co
just that they will no longer be going to school wit
there will be no more texting, no emails, no calls,
your innermost secrets and desires to. 'That friend
young while you grow up,' explains Nicky, 'it is as
abandoned you.' If the friend was killed in an accio
also involved in but survived, then once again the
enormous.

LOSS THROUGH SU

No one knows for sure why the suicide rate in you
so alarmingly, but it now accounts for 30% of dea
age group. In 2003, 334 young men and 92 your
group killed themselves in England (Source: Depa
2005) and suicide is now the second most com
young people after accidental death. Increased le
use of drugs such as alcohol and cannabis, family
stresses of modern life (not least the need to do
can all lead to a sense of hopelessness and desp

If you have lost a friend or sibling through suicide
and even years to come to terms with because, li
suicide is still a taboo subject. This means people
about it so you may not feel able to discuss how
you know – but you definitely *do* need to discuss
question in cases of suicide is 'why?': Why did th
they not come to me? Why didn't I know they felt
couldn't I stop them?

Because you get stuck in this never-ending search
not exist, the grieving process cannot progress un
someone who can help you to move on. This is i

feel very responsible if the other members of the family are coping badly. It's as though they feel they must take over the role of mum or dad even when they are in no emotional state to do so. There is a frantic need to 'hold the family together' and this perceived responsibility can be so stressful that it breeds resentment over the death. All the teenager really wants to do is to return to normal, but things will never be the same again and the grieving does not stop until they can accept this and the new circumstances of their life.

LOSS OF A SIBLING (BROTHER/SISTER)

There can also be resentment when a young person loses their only brother or sister, as Nicky Martin explains: 'If they are left as an only child they can feel huge responsibility to now be the "perfect" child for their parents and they may resent that.' If their sibling was their best friend and confidant, they may feel extremely isolated and lonely as well. This feeling will be even stronger if they shared a room with the sibling and must now sleep alone. If more than one brother or sister survives they may feel guilty if they seem to be getting over the death at different rates. 'If you are still grieving while your siblings have got over it you may think there is something wrong with you,' says Nicky. In addition you may feel guilty that you can't make the pain go away for your parents. In fact, on the death of a child, parents can sometimes get so lost in their own grief they unwittingly neglect the needs of their other children and this is where outside help, in the form of counselling or a bereavement group, can be very beneficial.

LOSS OF A FRIEND

When you are young, the last thing that ever enters your mind is that a friend will die before you. It can be a real shock, says Nicky Martin: 'You may have been planning things together and now that friend is gone. How are you meant to go back to school with the friend not there any more?' The loss of a friend can be all-consuming – it's not just that they will no longer be going to school with you, but also that there will be no more texting, no emails, no calls, no one to confide your innermost secrets and desires to. 'That friend will remain forever young while you grow up,' explains Nicky, 'it is as if they have abandoned you.' If the friend was killed in an accident which you were also involved in but survived, then once again the sense of guilt can be enormous.

LOSS THROUGH SUICIDE

No one knows for sure why the suicide rate in young people is rising so alarmingly, but it now accounts for 30% of deaths in the 15 to 24 age group. In 2003, 334 young men and 92 young women in this age group killed themselves in England (Source: Department of Health, 2005) and suicide is now the second most common cause of death in young people after accidental death. Increased levels of bullying, the use of drugs such as alcohol and cannabis, family break-up, and the stresses of modern life (not least the need to do well academically) can all lead to a sense of hopelessness and despair.

If you have lost a friend or sibling through suicide it can take months and even years to come to terms with because, like death itself, suicide is still a taboo subject. This means people are less likely to talk about it so you may not feel able to discuss how you feel with people you know – but you definitely *do* need to discuss it, because the big question in cases of suicide is 'why?': Why did they do this? Why did they not come to me? Why didn't I know they felt so bad? Why couldn't I stop them?

Because you get stuck in this never-ending search for answers that do not exist, the grieving process cannot progress until you talk to someone who can help you to move on. This is important because

American research has shown that if you have had a friend or relative die through suicide you are more likely to commit suicide yourself. It's almost as if the exposure to suicide influences young people who are in a vulnerable state to commit suicide themselves. If you have a friend who has been affected by suicide, Mind has an excellent booklet available entitled *How to help someone who is feeling suicidal* (see Chapter 10: Helpful organisations).

LOSS THROUGH AN ACT OF VIOLENCE

Like suicide, loss through an act of violence can have a devastating effect. We struggle to come to terms with something so unacceptable and so appalling to us. When someone we know is murdered we can't believe the unnecessary waste. Running through our minds may be the thought 'Why them? Why not me?' and conversely we may also feel guilty because we feel relieved that they were the victims and not us. For the many people bereaved by the terrorist bombings in London, trying to make sense of it all just intensifies the grief – because there is no sense. Once again, seeing a counsellor or joining a therapy group specifically set up for people in the same situation can be a real help.

ANTICIPATED LOSS THROUGH TERMINAL ILLNESS

Knowing someone you love is about to die doesn't mean you will not go through a grieving phase – of course you will. You may also feel some additional emotions. 'One of the things teenagers have said to me before a death in the family through illness is that they want to escape,' explains Nicky Martin. 'They don't want to be in the house with the dying person. They often feel guilty about it but it is totally understandable and normal. Having someone dying in the house, or a member of the family in a hospice, means the future is put on hold.' Siblings may feel jealous if a brother or sister has received a lot of attention during a terminal illness and this in turn can make them feel guilty. There is an in-depth look at death through terminal illness in Chapter 6.

WHO CAN I TURN TO?
The formal bodies you can turn to for help

Sharing your thoughts or feelings is vitally important to the grieving process. Many people feel like holding their grief close and deep inside themselves, but this will not make it grow any less painful or make it go away. However, sharing your experience of grief actually makes it easier to cope with – and in most cases, sharing means talking. If you have recently been bereaved you may feel very isolated and alone with your grief, but you'll be surprised at just how many people there are out there who can offer advice and support. The diagram on the next page lists some of the people you can talk to:

FAMILY MEMBERS AND FRIENDS

In most cases when someone we love or care for dies our first reaction is to turn to someone else we are close to for comfort. This could be a member of our family (such as a mother, father, sister or brother, aunt or uncle, or grandparent) or it could be a friend. Because they know us it is probable they were also acquainted with the person who has died and so can share common memories and stories about them. The subject of friends is covered in-depth in Chapter 5.

Who can I turn to?

However, some people find it very difficult to talk about their feelings, especially with those close to them, and get very embarrassed. If you are in this situation, you may find it easier to talk to someone you don't know, or anonymously over the phone or via a chatroom. There are many professional individuals and organisations that can offer support. These are outlined in the paragraphs below.

'You'll be surprised at just how many people there are out there who can offer advice and support.'

COUNSELLING

You may be wary of asking for counselling, but it really can help. B M Shaughnessy is a trained youth worker who specialises in crisis counselling. She has helped many young people who have been bereaved, especially those who have lost loved ones through accidents or through violence. 'In this age group you need to act fast because teenagers build up this tremendous barricade very quickly to protect themselves and to contain their pain,' she explains. 'They find loss deeply humiliating and embarrassing and they have to find a way to recover from that so you have to act quickly.' She describes the process of counselling as 'providing tools for the bereaved to deal with the immediate shock and the frightening aftermath, and then helping them find a way to internalise (take in and come to terms with) the loss of this person. It is a kind of 'resurrection' of the lost person inside the surviving person – it's as if they integrate the person who has died into themselves.'

What do counsellors do?

Different counsellors will use different methods, but B M Shaughnessy sees counselling as having three distinct stages.

- **First stage**: 'You have to deal with the immediate pain. If I see someone straight after the funeral I will ask them "what did you wear?" or "did you have lunch?". I try to get them talking about the event in a very practical way and this grounds them in the fact that it really has happened. These are trigger questions to help them collect themselves.'
- **Second stage**: Shaughnessy describes this stage as helping the bereaved person to find a symbolic action. The symbolic action, rite or ceremony has to mean something specific to the person involved for it to have any significance. In Chapter 6 we talk about symbolic actions in more detail, but Shaughnessy says many people feel better if they put something in the coffin. 'You can get someone

else to physically put it in for you,' she says; 'you don't have to do it yourself, but you do have to feel ready and able to do it. When his older brother died, one boy put a used football ticket from a game they had watched together in the coffin.' In the case of terminal illness you can begin the grieving process by doing something for your loved one before they die – this is covered in Chapter 7. 'Symbolic acts are a way to help you through the difficulty so they are very important in the symbolic recovery,' she says.

■ **Third stage**: 'This is the point when bereaved people know they are healing,' Shaughnessy says, 'when they find that missing person inside themselves again. You can just tell because there's a sort of peace about it and they start talking about the dead person in a more real way.' (You will find grieving teenagers' accounts of how they knew they had reached this stage in Chapter 8).

'Asking for advice or support doesn't mean you are weak or not coping – what it does mean is that you are taking positive steps to help yourself feel better.'

Who will benefit from counselling?

Even if you *can* talk to your family and friends, you may still find it useful to talk to someone you don't know, who has experience of bereavement counselling. Asking for their advice or support doesn't mean you are weak or not coping – what it does mean is that you are taking positive steps to help yourself feel better. If you feel you could benefit by talking to a bereavement counsellor, you could ask your doctor to put you in contact with a local counsellor or group. Alternatively, the rest of this chapter lists some of the organisations that can offer advice in the form of counsellors to talk to, leaflets and pamphlets to read, and interactive activities. Some of the websites contain real-life accounts written by young people who have been bereaved. Information and contact details for all the bodies mentioned can be found in Chapter 10.

TELEPHONE HELPLINES

Sometimes talking face to face can be difficult and talking to a sympathetic person on the end of a phone line may be easier. Here are of the helplines you could ring; further details are given in Chapter 10.

- **Childline (0800 1111)** is specifically set up for young people who wish to talk about their problems – anything from bullying to drug abuse. In the 2004/05 period Childline received 1905 calls and letters about bereavement from young people. Calls are confidential and free and you can contact Childline 24 hours a day on any day of the year. If you feel you do want to see someone in person then its counsellors can put you in contact with someone in your area.
- Some people think the **Samaritans (08457 909090)** exist solely to help those who are feeling suicidal – but in fact, the Samaritans are there to help anyone who is having difficulties with coping. They offer a confidential, 24-hour service and in 2003 received 4,800,000 calls, emails and letters (93% of contacts are made by phone).
- **CRUSE (0808 808 1677)** is an organisation dedicated to bereavement care and both its free helpline and its RD4U website are specifically for young people.
- **Winston's Wish (0845 20 30 40 5)** works with young people up to the age of 18 and offers support and advice.
- Although **Connexions (0808 00 13 2 19)** advisers are not trained counsellors they can talk you through what counselling is available.

SELF-HELP AND SUPPORT GROUPS

There are many national organisations that have been set up specifically to help the bereaved:

- The **Childhood Bereavement Network (www.ncb.org.uk/cbn)** lists support groups across the country and has other useful information.
- The **Childhood Bereavement Trust (www.childbereavement.org.uk)** is a charity helping young bereaved people and their families and offers videos and CD-ROMS that may prove useful.
- As stated above, **CRUSE (www.crusebereavementcare.org.uk)** has an area dedicated to young people and can help with finding counselling in your area.
- **Winston's Wish (www.winstonswish.org.uk)** works with young people individually and in groups and its website contains a 'For Young People' section with some very creative things to do to help make you feel better.
- In Scotland the **Notre Dame Centre (www.notredamecentre.org.uk)** offers a bereavement service specially aimed at young people and their families called RAFT (Recovery After Trauma) and a grief and loss peer support education programme for 6- to 18-year-olds called Seasons For Growth.

CHAPTER FIVE:

YOU'VE GOT A FRIEND

What friends can do to help and comfort you

It's in times of need that you find out who your real friends are – or that's how the saying goes. After a bereavement you will probably need your friends more than ever, yet you may find they don't seem to be there for you. This isn't because they think death is catching or because they don't care; it's because they feel awkward and don't know what to say. On one hand they may be worried that if they talk to you about the deceased person it will upset you, and on the other they might think that if they don't talk about them, they are showing no respect for the dead. Friends fret that they'll be too happy when you are sad, that you might take something they say the wrong way and, worst of all, that if you start crying they may cry too and distress you even more.

'After a bereavement you will probably need your friends more than ever, yet you may find they don't seem to be there for you.'

However, real friends will get beyond this awkwardness and many will want to help in any way they can. The danger is that they will try to smother you with kindness and, no matter how well-meant their efforts may be, they could end up doing more harm then good. If you have a friend who really wants to help, try asking them to read through this chapter. If you are that friend, here are some of the things your grieving friend might be thinking ...

'GIVE ME SPACE'

When a person is grieving they often need time by themselves. It doesn't mean they are no longer your friend – just that there are things they need to sort out in their own mind. Sometimes they may want to discuss these with you; other times they will want to keep things to themselves, and you should give them the space to do this. You should also respect their physical space: whereas some people find great comfort in physical contact such as hugs, others can't bear to be touched. 'It isn't that you are being rejected,' explains counsellor Nicky Martin: 'it probably has more to do with the fact that they are afraid it will make them cry and they don't want you to see them break down.'

'LAUGH WITH ME AND CRY WITH ME'

On the other hand, crying with them may be exactly what your friend wants and needs. By sharing the emotion – be it laughing or crying – you are normalising it and helping them to feel less lonely. The most important milestones and times of our lives are those we celebrate with an emotional sharing – the birth of a child, a wedding and, of course, a funeral – and it is amazing how cathartic (cleansing and therapeutic) these emotional outpourings can be.

'LET'S DO NORMAL STUFF TOGETHER'

Many people feel they are in limbo after losing someone they love, so getting back to a normal routine is a way for them to 'get on with life'. If your friend asks you to go shopping, to go to football, to see a film or to go to a disco with them, they are not being callous or unfeeling towards the person they have lost; it is because, in an uncertain world, these normal activities are something they know and can hold on to.

'BEWARE OF MY MOODINESS'

Considering the emotional stress bereaved people experience it's no surprise that you may find yourself on the receiving end of their mood swings. 'They may well get grumpy, or get annoyed more than they ever did before,' explains Nicky Martin. 'Try to understand that it's not you the grumpiness is aimed at; it's all part of the fact that they are not in control of their emotions, so don't take offence – just stick with them while they go through this phase.'

'DON'T FEEL SORRY FOR ME'

There's nothing worse for a grieving young person than to feel that he or she is an object of pity. It not only embarrasses them – it also makes them feel angry. This is a time when all they really want to do is get back to normal and be treated like everybody else, so they may also be thinking ...

'DON'T TREAT ME LIKE A LEPER'

When you are grieving you don't have some horrible disease – death is not catching. John or Jay are still the same friends they were before they lost their loved one, so treat them in that way. Leave the door open for them to come and talk to you or hang out with you if they need to. Although it is good to acknowledge that they may need to spend a lot of time with their families, sometimes getting out of that environment and being with friends can be a welcome relief.

'BE PATIENT WITH ME'

'Friends should be patient because many bereaved teenagers don't feel patient with themselves,' says Nicky Martin. 'They probably just want this awful feeling to go away as quickly as possible – but everyone grieves at their own speed.' While in the modern world it seems everyone wants to get the business of death and bereavement out of the way as quickly as possible, grief will not be hurried so a little patience on your part will be much appreciated.

'WATCH OUT FOR ME'

It's not just adults who turn to drink and drugs to help them through difficult times – some young people do, too. Using alcohol, nicotine or even cannabis to 'numb the pain' can actually make things worse because it cuts short the natural grieving process and doesn't take the pain away. According to the Department of Health, in 2003 cannabis was the most frequently reported illicit drug, used by 26% of 16- to 24-year-olds. But drug use can lead to severe health and mental problems. In fact, according to the charity Mind, the increase in drug misuse is likely to have contributed to the rise in suicide rates in the young. If a bereaved friend starts exhibiting self-destructive behaviour in the form of alcohol abuse or any other drug abuse then they need help quickly. If you can't talk to them about it, you must tell an adult or get in contact with one of the support groups listed in Chapter 10 of this book.

For a closer look at issues related to addictions
see *Real Life Issues: Addictions*

If you notice a bereaved friend is not eating properly, not bathing or
not changing their clothes regularly, it could be the onset of depression
(see Chapter 2). This should be addressed as soon as possible. If you
can't get your friend to talk about the situation you must make sure an
adult is aware of what is going on.

'PLEASE LISTEN TO ME'

Bereaved people often need to talk through what they are feeling
again and again, and if you are a true friend you will be willing to sit
and listen to them. Sometimes, they won't even need you to answer –
they just need to get what is troubling them off their chests. This is
especially true when young people have been bereaved, because
adults often mistakenly think they shouldn't talk about the dead person
in front of them for fear of causing upset. What is actually upsetting is
the kind of 'erasure' of the dead person that this causes. Your friend
was close to their loved one, so of course they want to talk about
them.

'LET'S TALK HONESTLY'

One of the worst things people will do after a death is begin to talk in
clichés, for example referring to 'the person who has passed on' in the
third person. Your friendship will be much more appreciated if you are
honest and direct. Mention the person who has died by name, or say
'your dad' or 'your mum' – don't try to leave them out of the
conversation and don't be afraid to talk about the death; this terrible
thing has happened and it shouldn't be ignored. Try to encourage your
friend to talk about the person who has died and share stories if you
knew them too.

'JUST BE THERE FOR ME'

Ultimately, the best thing you can do for a grieving friend is to be there for them. Many young bereaved people feel extremely isolated in their grief, and just knowing that you care will be comforting. Even a simple text asking 'How are you doing today?', an email or a quick call will be very supportive, as will offers to do school research or homework together. You don't need to make grand gestures and more often than not it is the little things you do that are the most appreciated.

'Many young bereaved people feel extremely isolated in their grief, and just knowing that you care will be comforting.'

CHAPTER SIX:

HOW CAN I HELP MYSELF?
Things you can do to help yourself through the mourning process

When your world has been turned upside down by the loss of someone you love, it's sometimes hard to organise your thoughts. More often than not just managing to get up, get dressed and get through the day is as much as you can do. However, if you can focus outside this terrible bubble of pain you exist in, even for a little while, there are positive steps and activities you can undertake to help lessen that pain – you may not believe it, but it's true. Some of the activities listed in this chapter can be shared with other people who have been affected by the bereavement too (such as siblings if you have lost a parent), bringing you all closer together.

'If you can focus outside this terrible bubble of pain you exist in, even for a little while, there are positive steps and activities you can undertake to help lessen that pain.'

Before we get to the practical self-help activities, the biggest thing you can do to help yourself heal is to allow yourself to ...

FEEL THE PAIN

In a society where males are told that 'big boys don't cry' and public displays of grief are often deemed unseemly or improper, many of us internalise (shut in) our grief, maintaining what appears to be a 'dignified' silence. But grief should not be silenced – it should be released, so give yourself **permission to grieve**. Remember to:

■ **Cry if you want to**. Don't try and be 'strong' for the people around you. You need to do what's right for you. Yes, your crying may set off other people, but shared tears can also be healing tears. Recent public shows of mourning such as the memorials after 9/11 and after the London tube bombings have been cathartic occasions, allowing everyone to come to terms with these appalling events. If you are embarrassed about crying in public then make sure you have a private space where you can go to shed your tears.

■ **Let yourself be angry**. Anger can sometimes be scary; it's an emotion that can make us feel completely out of control. But don't suppress it, let it out. It doesn't matter if you are angry with the person who has died for leaving you, with God for letting them die, or at the world in general: your anger is real so you must acknowledge it. What you must not do is let the anger spill over into harm against yourself or other people. When it gets too much, throw some cushions around, or even punch them. Scream as hard as you can into a pillow, or put on some loud dance music and dance the anger out. In fact, exercise of any kind helps to relieve anger, and we will explore this in more detail in the 'Work it out' section of this chapter.

- **Look after yourself**. Chapter 2 of this book described some of the physical and emotional symptoms of grief. You will be better able to cope with these if you make sure you eat well, get enough sleep and keep tabs on your general health. Grief makes us feel fragile, so make sure you treat yourself gently.

IT'S GOOD TO TALK

 They say a problem shared is a problem halved, and just getting things off your chest really can make you feel lighter in spirit. Some people feel the need to see a specialised counsellor but for many, just talking to someone they know can help. You could try:

- Someone close to you – a parent, sibling, aunt or uncle or a friend
- A teacher at school you particularly like
- Your school counsellor (if there is one)
- A drop-in centre for youth counselling in your area
- Your local vicar or priest, Rabbi, Imam or other spiritual adviser (if you have a religious belief)
- Speaking to someone anonymously via a helpline.

These options are explored more fully in Chapters 4 and 5. If you really feel you aren't coping, then arrange a visit to your doctor to find a bereavement group you could join.

Talk about anything and everything. Describe your feelings and your fears, however trivial they may seem. Talk about the person who has died, reminisce about them, about their favourite films or bands and their other likes and dislikes. If you can't face that then talk about school and any problems you might be having. You may find talking out loud to the person who has died helps as well. Find yourself a private spot and tell them how much you love them, tell them how much you miss them; if you are angry then say so and explain why, and let them know how you are doing. Whatever else you do to help yourself just make sure you *talk*.

PUT IT ON PAPER

 Writing our thoughts down makes them seem more real, more concrete. Even if you never show your writing to another soul, *you* know it is there in black and white. If you like writing, here are a few ideas that can really help:

- **Write a letter to the person who has died**. Include all those things you never quite got around to saying while they were alive. Tell them you love them and that you miss them. If the letter gives you comfort, then leave it unsealed and put it somewhere handy where you can get to it and read it back whenever you wish. If you are not yet ready to reread the letter then seal it in an envelope or secure with a ribbon or piece of string, then put it away somewhere safe, in a drawer or box. You will know you are on the road to recovery when you feel able to open the letter and read it again.

- **Keep a diary**. This is a great way for you to monitor your feelings on a day-to-day basis and is also like having a secret friend you can confide in. If something has made you feel sad then write about it, or if someone said something really nice, make sure you include it. Do put in things that seem mundane – even the greatest diarists write about little, everyday details such as listing what they ate for supper. If you experience weird or disturbing dreams then keep a dream diary. You remember dreams most vividly just as you wake up, so put a pen and notebook on your bedside table and write down what you can remember of your dream when you awaken. You may well find certain themes or

symbols keep appearing and they may be pointers to things that
are troubling you.

- **Write a poem**. Some of the most beautiful poetry has been
  written to or for people who have died. Like love, death moves
  humans emotionally and these emotions can trigger off bouts of
  tremendous creative inspiration. You may not be a great poet, but if
  you find writing a poem helps you to express your feelings, that's a
  good thing.

- **Rip up notes**. If you are experiencing really negative or hurtful
  thoughts ('I'm so angry' or 'I hate you for leaving me') then write
  them down on a piece of paper. Now rip the paper into shreds and
  throw the pieces in the bin – or, if you have the facilities, burn them
  in a fire. Imagine the negative thoughts being released as the
  smoke rises.

DRAW A PICTURE

Many counsellors use art therapy to help younger bereaved
children – the use of coloured pencils and crayons allows
them to express what they are feeling even if they haven't
got the words for it. However, drawing pictures can be
therapeutic whatever your age. Often it helps to draw a
picture of the dead person as you would like to see them – happy and
smiling, or in a situation or place they particularly liked. You could also
draw them surrounded by loved ones, including yourself.

One technique Nicky Martin finds particularly helpful is to make a
photo collage. Draw a picture of the deceased person and stick it
onto a larger piece of card or noticeboard. Then cut out pictures
from magazines that remind you of that person (a favourite place, or
their favourite band or film) and stick them around the picture. You
could also hunt through old photographs of the person and stick
these on the board too. You can keep your collage all for yourself or

you can make a family one, asking other people to add their own pictures.

MAKE MUSIC

Music is wonderfully evocative: hearing a piece of music you particularly like can send you on a powerful memory rush right back to the first time and place you heard it. Music can also remind you of certain people – which is why, at funerals, special care is usually taken by the family to choose music that their loved one enjoyed listening to. As a tribute to the person who has died and also to make you feel closer to them, you could make a tape or a CD of all their favourite tracks. Make sure you clearly label it ('____'s special CD' or 'In Memory of ____'). You don't need to listen to it if you don't want to but you could place the CD in a memory box dedicated to the person who has died (see below).

CREATE A MEMORY BOX

Like the photo collage, this is something you can do alone or with your family or friends – whichever seems the most appropriate. Collect things that remind you of the person who has died or personal things that belonged to them – for example:

- Jewellery or clothing
- Books
- Photographs
- Trinkets
- Toys
- Letters they have written
- Pictures they have drawn

- Mementoes from shared holidays (shells, stones, ticket stubs)
- Football paraphernalia, if they were a fan
- An empty bottle of their favourite scent.

Now put it all into a box, one you have bought especially for the occasion or even an old shoebox you have decorated yourself. Clearly mark the box with the name of the person who has died and every time you feel like it, open the box to go through these wonderful memories you have of them.

WORK IT OUT

 It has now been clinically proven that exercising can help relieve depression. The main reason for this is that exercise boosts the body's levels of the brain hormone serotonin, which is responsible for regulating our moods, appetite and sleep cycles. Another physical reason why exercise is such a good depression-buster is that it disperses the build-up of stress-inducing chemicals such as adrenalin. From an emotional point of view exercise can raise self-esteem and, because much exercise is team-orientated, it gives us social stimulus. So if you feel up to it, do play football or another team sport, or join an exercise class such as dance, aerobics or body pump. If you would rather exercise alone, many bereaved people find swimming very helpful and relaxing (imagine all your pain travelling through your fingertips and toes out into the water to be washed away). Other good exercises to undertake alone or with a friend are power walking (especially through parks or open countryside where you can really stride out) and cycling through the countryside. Try to exercise two to five times a week but don't get obsessive about it – exercise will not burn the pain away, only help to relieve it.

CREATE YOUR OWN SYMBOLIC ACTION

Although you may have been to the deceased person's funeral service and gained comfort through it, you may still feel you want to give them your own special ceremony as a tribute. If the deceased person was not particularly religious and therefore did not have any kind of funeral rite, you may also wish to hold a ceremony as your own mark of respect. Counsellor B M Shaughnessy says: 'Religions seem to have co-opted this (aspect of grieving). In my work I discovered that memorials are very important – it always seems to heal something when a symbolic action or form is found.'

B M Shaughnessy had one young client who took one of his dead father's shirts to wear in bed after he had died in an accident. When he felt he had reached a stage in his mourning when it was appropriate, he was helped to ritually burn the shirt on a bonfire in his father's memory, symbolically letting his father go and letting go of his own pain. When the actor River Phoenix died, a teenage friend took out his classic film My Own Private Idaho and sat watching it surrounded by lit tea lights. This was her symbolic action to his memory. Your own symbolic action can be anything you think of – but here are some ideas:

■ **Create a special place.** You can create your own special place for the deceased person where you keep a copy of their picture, a

'Memorials are very important – it always seems to heal something when a symbolic action or form is found.'

B M Shaughnessy

votive candle (representing your devotion), incense sticks and some kind of small trinket or memento that reminds you of them. Here you can sit quietly, light the candle and incense and remember them (this could also be the special place you go to talk to them).

■ **Hold a feast**. You could serve all the deceased's favourite foods and invite guests to reminisce about times they spent with them. If you feel up to it, bake a special cake to mark the occasion. Each guest can then take a piece of the cake away with them. You could also make menus or place names with the date and the event on them for people to keep as a memento of the occasion.

■ **Create a garden.** Memorial gardens are now very popular because they are a lasting and beautiful reminder of the person. If the deceased loved flowers then you could hold a ceremony where you plant bulbs and seeds in their memory.

■ **Plant a tree.** Like a memorial garden, a tree is also a lasting memorial to a loved one and can be planted ceremonially.

■ **Have a special 'remembrance' evening.** If you have lost a friend then get together with other friends and celebrate their life. Sit together, preferably in a circle, and one by one read out letters, poems or quotes that you have written for them, or you feel have special meaning. You could also listen to songs they liked.

■ **Return to a special place.** If you have lost a member of your family you may like to return as a group to a place that holds special memories for you (such as a holiday location or somewhere you used to go on walks together) and then take it in turns to talk about happy times you have spent there with your loved one.

VISUALISATIONS

Earlier in this chapter we talked about how exercise can help while you are grieving. Many people find that exercises meant to relax you (such as yoga, t'ai chi and even meditation) are beneficial too, not only because they can calm you mentally but also because the breathing techniques involved offer relief from stress. If you feel these could help, then join a class.

However, if you don't yet feel up to meeting lots of other people, one very simple form of meditation you can do by yourself is 'visualisation', which involves picturing images in your mind. You don't need any special equipment or training and you'll find the more you do it, the easier visualisation becomes.

To start, lie or sit somewhere comfortable in a quiet, darkened room. Make sure you are warm enough and your clothes are loose and soft. Close your eyes. Now start breathing deeply and slowly – in through your nose and out through your mouth – and become aware if any of your muscles are tense. If so, consciously clench them for a second or two before releasing them. When you feel perfectly relaxed, start the visualisation. The headings below explain what to do next.

Visualisation for well-being or wholeness

In your mind's eye see your body lying down and imagine a source of light similar to the sun or moon above you. Imagine pure silver light cascading down onto your body. The light enters through the top of your head and then courses down through your body to your toes. When it reaches your toes, imagine it washing straight back up to your head again. As your body is filled with this brilliant light you feel yourself being cleansed and renewed, healed and revived. You'll know when to stop because you will feel the energy in the light source is waning, so now imagine the light source switching itself off in order to rebuild its power.

Visualisation for removing negative thoughts

Imagine all those negative thoughts running wild in your head. Now picture a white, fluffy cloud hovering above your head. Shoot all those angry, hurtful thoughts through your skull straight into the cloud and watch it get blacker and blacker as they fill it up. Now see a puff of wind taking the cloud away from you, out over a large sea or lake – then watch as the negative thoughts rain down into the water to be washed away, leaving the cloud pure and white again.

Visualisation for peace of mind

This is especially good if you find you just can't stop your mind from going over and over things, as if you have a load of useless chatter in your brain and you can't shut it up. Think of your body as a telephone exchange. See all the cables going in and out of your body – down each one is travelling yet another voice that won't shut up. Now imagine you have a pair of large scissors in your hands and cut through the cables one by one, hearing each go silent as you do so. By the time you cut the last cable you are surrounded by peace and quiet.

Visualisation to help you sleep

Of course, the most famous sleep visualisation is counting sheep jumping over a fence – but these ones are much more fun! Just decide which of the images – stars in space or a fabulous underwater grotto – appeals to you more and then follow that visualisation.

■ **Shooting to the stars.** Imagine yourself as a rocket, tall and straight. You are being shot up through the atmosphere, travelling up, up into space, out past the Moon and Mars. As you travel further and further away from Earth and all your worries you feel yourself become lighter and lighter. With your troubles behind you, you are free to enjoy the silence and brilliance of the stars. You feel safe here, bathed in their light, and now you can sleep.

■ **Diving into the sea.** See yourself as a mermaid or merman, diving from a rock into a fabulously warm clear sea. As you dive through the water, feel its silkiness on your skin and watch the dolphins and brightly coloured fish around you. There are no sharks here, just beautiful creatures. The further down you dive the heavier you get with the warm water caressing you. Your movements get slower and slower until you glide into a shady underwater grotto where you feel completely safe. The dappled sunlight from the surface makes you feel drowsy and you sleep.

As you get better at it, try adding your own details and making up your own visualisations using images that especially appeal to you. Once a visualisation is over, allow yourself a little time to come back to reality. Open your eyes, realise where you are and then sit up slowly.

AFFIRMATIONS

Affirmations are simply sayings that reaffirm positive thought processes. What they do is to break the negative thought patterns that grief can push us into, such as 'I'm never going to be happy again' or 'I can never make it better'. The most famous affirmation, 'every day, in every way, I am getting better and better', was used with great success by the patients of French clinician Emil Coue in the 1920s. He made them repeat this affirmation several times each day and they actually did get better.

You can say affirmations as you lie in bed just after waking or just before going to sleep. In order to remind yourself of them, write your personal affirmations out on a piece of paper or card and place them where you will see them daily, for example by slipping them into the frame of a mirror or pinning them onto a bedroom wall. The more you repeat the affirmations the more they will stick with you, replacing negative thought patterns. You can choose from the general affirmations below or, even better, make up your own. Remember that they have to emphasise the positive – the negative is banned. Because of this you can't have affirmations that start 'I will not ...' Here are some examples:

'My future is bright, safe, and loving.'

'I give myself permission to take all the time I need to heal.'

'I give myself permission to grieve as long as I need to.'

'My grief grows smaller day by day as I grow stronger.'

'I let go of grief and guilt.'

'My body is filled with light and strength.'

'I deserve to be happy and healthy.'

'I am surrounded by love. I am safe.'

'Every day, in every way, I am getting better.'

CHAPTER SEVEN:

PREPARING FOR A DEATH TO COME
How to prepare for an expected bereavement

Living with someone who you know is dying can put an intolerable strain on you. You may feel you always need to be happy and positive around them however bad you feel inside. You may not wish to mention the illness and you may feel resentful that your life has been put on hold until the inevitable happens. You and your family may also experience 'anticipatory grief', which feels as if you are already grieving for a person who has not yet died and may mean you go through all the stages of grief – denial, anger, sadness, anxiety. The worst thing you can do is try to ignore this; you and your family need to acknowledge it.

'Whatever else you do, remember the time you have with this person is precious, so be there for them and be as honest as you can with yourself and with them.'

GETTING SUPPORT

Some people with terminal illnesses stay at home until their death and, as mentioned in Chapter 3, this can make the other members of the household feel trapped. You may resent all the attention this person is getting and feel they have 'taken over' your home and so getting out of the house or 'escaping' somewhere else becomes important to you. This may make you feel guilty but, as counsellor Nicky Martin explains, it is totally understandable and normal. It is also normal to feel you are stuck in a time bubble until the person dies. 'Having someone dying in the house and not wanting to look to the future is at odds with the way teenagers usually feel, because for them the future is everything,' says Nicky. If the sick person is a sibling you may feel jealous at all the attention they are receiving while your needs seem to have been sidelined. However, there is now excellent counselling available both for the terminally ill person themselves and for their families. Organisations such as Winston's Wish and Cruse can offer real support (see Chapter 4).

Even if the ill person does not go into a hospice, many now provide their facilities as a 'home hospice', in which nurses and counsellors perform care services in the person's own home. However, many terminally ill people do go into hospices. Far from being institutional and depressing, modern hospices are light, welcoming places with excellent facilities, and patients and their families have a very positive response to the experience. This is because the ill person receives constant medical attention, including pain relief, while counselling is available not only to the person who is ill but also to the family. Counselling is given both before and after the person's death and this can really help in dealing with anticipatory grief as well as the grief after the loss.

THINGS FOR YOU TO DO

Among the things many young people have said to crisis counsellor
B M Shaughnessy after the death of a loved one are 'I wish I had said
this' or 'I wish I had done that'. In the case of a terminal illness, you still
have the chance to say and do things that you need to say and do.
Many people hesitate before doing so because they are waiting for the
'perfect moment' – but the truth is, that moment may never come and
you need to act before your time with this person runs out. You may
also hesitate because you fear what their reaction will be. However,
there are strategies you can adopt to allay these fears.

Things to be said

Remember, this person may not be with you for much longer, so get it
clear in your head the things you want to say to them before they die.
The three main things most people need to express are:

- **'I love you.'** It's strange, but often the people we love the most are
  those we forget to tell we do. It's as if we take it for granted or are
  embarrassed by it. Telling someone you love them actually tells
  them a lot more. It says 'I care for you, respect and appreciate you
  and all you do for me, and I will miss you so badly when you are
  gone'. If you really do find it impossible to say 'I love you' out loud,
  write a letter telling them how much you love them. Alternatively
  you could make a cassette of you saying 'I love you' for them to
  listen to in private. But saying it to their face will make you feel so
  much better.
- **'I forgive you.'** There may be painful things you want to get off
  your chest, not least your anger that this person is about to leave
  you – so saying that you forgive them can be a very cathartic
  experience.

■ **'Please forgive me.'** By the same token, there may be things you
have said or done in the past that you feel were unfair or unkind
and, by asking their forgiveness, it's as if you are settling up your
account so that there is no unfinished business before their death.

Things to be done

In the same way that symbolic acts after someone has died can act as
a step forward or a breaking through, symbolic acts *before* the death
can help you through the grieving process. An example of this was two
sisters whose mother was dying from cancer. They really wanted to do
something for her so they went and sorted out all her clothes, colour-
coding them in her wardrobe and drawers. This was their symbolic act.
One girl knitted her gran a pair of thick socks after she complained of
permanently frozen feet. Here are some ideas of other things you
could do for or with your loved one:

■ **Organising.** Help them sort through their jewellery/make-up box or
catalogue their CD collection with them. Make sure all their favourite
T-shirts and other clothes are washed and ready for them.
■ **Pampering..** Help them apply make-up. Give them a foot or hand
massage. Paint your nails and toenails together or paint theirs for
them. If their hair has not been affected by chemotherapy, offer to
wash it for them and style it.
■ **Remembering.** Make them a scrapbook of sporting memorabilia
featuring their favourite team. Start a memory box with them
including photographs, drawings, trinkets, articles cut from
magazines on their favourite bands/sports teams/film stars/holiday
destinations. Make a photo-collage of pictures of you together, of
family, and of other people who are important in your lives. Add
personal drawings or pictures they especially like cut from
magazines.

■ **Recording.** Burn them a CD or download new tracks you think they may like. Make a home film for them. Get friends and members of the family to talk to camera about happy times and events from the past and include footage of the person who is ill with you and the family. If there is a family pet, get footage of the pet too. If they wish to record a final message or make a film then help by making sure they have access to a recorder or camera and the necessary tapes or cassettes (one woman made tapes of messages to be played by each of her three children when they reached 18 years old).

Whatever else you do, remember that the time you have with this person is precious, so be there for them and be as honest as you can with yourself and with them.

CHAPTER EIGHT:

MOVING ON
How to spot when you are healing

When you are caught in a grief that dominates your world it is difficult to believe that this pain might one day ease. But sooner or later it does and in most cases the bereaved person knows they are healing. As B M Shaughnessy puts it, 'you have to reach the point where you put the missing person in the past and you in the present.' This doesn't mean you forget this person – far from it. 'People say things like "in a few years you'll hardly ever remember", whereas I think it is important to give them permission to never forget,' says Shaughnessy. 'What they should be saying is "never, ever forget this person because they were very important to you".' What happens is not that you forget but that you accept that your loved one is gone and find a way of getting on with your own life.

REAL-LIFE EXPERIENCES

The next page lists some of the ways other bereaved people have finally realised they are healing and moving on:

'Tommy's favourite song came on the radio the other day. Normally, that would make me feel sad because he's not around to hear it any more, but that day it made me smile because I remembered the first time we heard it together and that was a happy time.'

'The day I woke up and thoughts of my dead mum weren't the first thing to go through my head was the day I realised I was getting over it. What I actually thought about was wow, look at the sun shining through the curtains, it's going to be a lovely day.'

'A friend asked me to go to her birthday disco and, instead of feeling guilty about going out and enjoying myself, I found myself getting really excited.'

'I recently sat my GCSEs and got really good grades. Although I was sad that dad wasn't around to congratulate me all I kept thinking was "boy he would have been proud of me", and that made me feel all warm inside.'

'We hadn't been on holiday as a family since Sally died — none of us felt like it. But when mum suggested it and brought the brochures home we all started talking over each other just like we used to when Sally was alive. That made us laugh; she would have enjoyed that.'

'For a while after my brother died I couldn't bear to watch sad films on the tv because they always made me cry. But I watched Jack Frost the other day, where Michael Keaton dies and comes back as a snowman and I didn't cry once. I felt comforted by it.'

'A mate told a really corny joke the other day and it made me laugh out loud, and I realised I couldn't remember laughing at anything since my auntie died.'

'I'm starting at a new school next term. Just after my bereavement the thought of meeting all those new people filled me with dread. Now I'm looking forward to it.'

'It's coming up to mum's birthday and last year that was a terrible time as we all missed her so much. This year, we still miss her — but dad's taking us all out for dinner in her honour. I think she would really have appreciated that. It's going to be a celebration.'

'I used to get really angry with myself for crying at school, but all my friends and teachers have been so brilliant about it and I very rarely feel like crying now — and if I do I know they'll understand.'

'I was having real problems with my school work; I just couldn't concentrate or get interested in anything. Then in English the other day, I suddenly realised I had totally lost myself in the subject and was really enjoying it. It was as if my brain had woken up again.'

A GRADUAL PROCESS

Moving on is a gradual process and there may be days when you have setbacks and find yourself experiencing that awful, shocking grief all over again. But you'll find these bouts get fewer and farther apart. You may notice a pattern to them: counsellor Nicky Martin explained in Chapter 2 that major dates might trigger relapses. These might include:

- First Christmas
- First birthday
- First anniversary of the death
- Milestones such as getting into university, passing your driving test, getting married or having your first child.

She advises you to 'try to put contingency plans in place – such as having someone special to talk to, or having something specific to do – for those times'.

When you do reach the 'moving on' phase, there are practical things you can do that can really help. This will probably be the first time since the bereavement that you feel like going out and meeting new people and feel strong enough to take positive action. For instance, after the death of her mother, one young client of Nicky's explained that there was now no one to cook for the family – they were surviving on takeaway pizza. So she enrolled in cookery classes, which made her

'You have to reach the point where you put the missing person in the past and you in the present.'

B M Shaughnessy

feel she was contributing to the well-being of her family and gave her a new interest. 'The important thing is to let young people know that it's OK to let normality back into their lives,' Nicky explains. 'It's OK to listen to new bands and go to new movies. It's OK to take an interest in magazines and in new clothes.' In fact, getting a new interest or hobby such as joining a gym or local football team, enrolling in art classes or taking up yoga are all beneficial things to do (see Chapter 6).

CHAPTER NINE: CONCLUSION

No one and nothing can make the pain, sadness and anguish of bereavement magically disappear. There is nothing anyone can say or do that will instantly relieve what a bereaved person goes through. In fact, going through it, or getting through it, to finally emerge the other side is the only way to grieve. In a society that no longer has time for protracted mourning periods, where you are meant to get over a death the minute the funeral service has ended, people have forgotten how to mourn, and even more importantly, why they need to mourn. Mourning gives us the space to feel and to express all the emotions the death of a loved one provokes – the anger, loss, sorrow, guilt, fear and vulnerability. We need to express these feelings in order to set them free, to let them go. That does not mean we should forget the person we have loved – as B M Shaughnessy says, 'forgetfulness isn't a healing position'. Instead, we should give ourselves permission to remember them, but also to move on, and through doing so, allow ourselves to heal.

This book exists to help with that healing process. The practical advice it contains is to give you or your family and friends ideas as to how to work through the bereavement process. Having reached this stage you

> *'Mourning gives us the space to feel and to express all the emotions the death of a loved one provokes – the anger, loss, sorrow, guilt, fear and vulnerability.'*

should be well aware that all you are experiencing and feeling is absolutely normal for a bereaved person. However, it is important to remember that this present 'normal' will not be a carbon copy of the 'normal' from your past. You will have learned things from the experience, many of them positive rather than negative. What many people take from the process of being bereaved is the realisation that life isn't forever: we all have a finite time here, and so we should never waste a moment of it. As Gandhi said, 'Live as if you were to die tomorrow.' With that in mind, here are some thoughts for you:

- Are there things you need to say to people that you haven't said? Maybe now would be a good time to say them.
- Are there things you want to do but have never got round to? Why not start them now?
- Give yourself permission to be happy and to enjoy life. Have fun.
- Be gentle with yourself; you've been through, or are going through, a lot.
- Repeat this affirmation daily: **'My future is safe and bright and I get better every day.'**

There is life after bereavement and you will know when you feel able and ready to start living it.

CHAPTER TEN:

HELPFUL ORGANISATIONS

The following organisations have a lot of experience in helping young people who have been bereaved and are able to offer practical and emotional advice. Some offer counselling as well as pamphlets and booklets on many aspects of bereavement.

ORGANISATIONS

CALM (Campaign Against Living Miserably)

Tel: 0800 585858 (Daily from 5pm to 3am)

www.thecalmzone.net

CALM is targetted specifically at young men aged between 15 and 35, but anyone can call their helpline and their website has two areas that may be of particular interest: 'Worried about someone else?' offers advice on how to talk to someone who is experiencing difficulties, while 'How have others coped?' contains first-hand experiences from people who have been bereaved. There are currently three 'CALMzones' around the country in Manchester, Merseyside and Bedfordshire, but you can call them wherever you live and they will put you in touch with nationally available services. CALM's advisors are all trained in counselling and the service is confidential.

Child Bereavement Trust

Aston House

West Wycombe

High Wycombe

Buckinghamshire HP14 3AG

Tel: 0845 357 1000

www.childbereavement.org.uk

This national UK charity started in 1994 and works to help young
people and their families. It has a wide range of books, videos,
CD-ROMS and information leaflets. There is a section titled 'For Young
People' on the website.

Childhood Bereavement Network

8 Wakley Street

London EC1V 7QF

Tel: 020 7843 6309

www.ncb.org.uk/cbn

Hosted by the National Children's Bureau, this excellent resource gives
local and national information on bereavement. On the website you
can find support in your area by clicking on the 'Open Access Service
Directory' and searching under your county.

Childline

Freepost 1111

London N1 0BR

Tel: 0800 1111

Textphone: 0800 400 222

www.childline.org.uk

If you can't talk to anyone you know about what you are feeling but
need to discuss things with someone, then you should contact
Childline. It takes young people's problems seriously and calls are
confidential. Its counsellors can offer advice about your local sources

of help. Check out the website where there is a downloadable information sheet (number 7) on bereavement. The telephone service is free and available 24/7.

Connexions
Tel: 0808 001 3219
Text: 07766 413 219
Textphone: 0800 0968 336
www.connexions-direct.com
Connexions advisers are not trained counsellors but they can talk you through what counselling is available. You can speak to a personal adviser at your local Connexions Centre. To find your local centre click on the 'Local Services' icon in the footer of the homepage or check out your local phone book.

Cruse Bereavement Care
Young People's helpline: 0808 808 1677 (freephone)
Day by Day helpline: 0870 167 1677
www.crusebereavementcare.org.uk
www.rd4u.org.uk
Email: helpline@crusebereavementcare.org.uk
Anyone can contact Cruse if they want to talk about bereavement. Its excellent website has a dedicated area for young people called 'RD4U', which has been designed by young people for young people and is full of helpful hints and tips. The website also lists publications that may prove useful.

Mind
Tel: 0845 766 0163
www.mind.org.uk
Mind is the leading mental health charity in England and Wales. Its website contains links to many articles on various aspects of

bereavement. It has centres throughout the country and you can use the website to find your nearest one. If you are worried that a friend may have suicidal tendencies then its booklet How to help someone who is feeling suicidal *may be useful.*

Notre Dame Centre
20 Athole Gardens
Glasgow G12 9BA
Tel: 0141 339 2366
www.notredamecentre.org.uk
The Notre Dame centre in Scotland offers a bereavement service called **RAFT (Recovery After Trauma)**, *which is specially aimed at young people and their families and is available immediately after the bereavement and beyond. For more information on RAFT, email raft@notredamecentre.org.uk.*

Notre Dame also offers **Seasons For Growth**, *which is a grief and loss peer support education programme. Aimed at 6- to 18-year-olds, it promotes resilience and offers coping resources through three areas: communication, decision-making and problem-solving. For more information, email sfg@notredamecentre.org.uk.*

RAFT (Recovery After Trauma)
See Notre Dame Centre.

Samaritans
Tel: 08457 909090
Textphone: 08457 909192
www.samaritans.org.uk
The Samaritans offer a confidential 24-hour service for anyone who wants to talk to one of their trained operators.

Seasons for growth

See Notre Dame Centre.

Winston's Wish

Clara Burgess Centre

Bayshill Road

Cheltenham GL50 3AW

Tel: 0845 20 30 40 5

www.winstonswish.org.uk

Winston's Wish has a very child-friendly approach and works with young people up to the age of 18. It can work with individual children or groups and offers support and advice. There is an excellent 'For young people' section on its website with fun and creative things you can do to help yourself to feel better and to heal. It also produces a range of publications on bereavement.

YoungMinds

48–50 St John's Street

London EC1M 4DG

Tel: 020 7336 8445

www.youngminds.org.uk

This national charity is committed to improving the mental health of all young people. It issues a magazine, YoungMinds, *as well as leaflets and booklets to help young people including one on general depression. There are a number of articles concerning bereavement on the website, and if you click on to the 'Info' Section you will find links to other organisations that can help in the case of bereavement.*

BOOKS

Trotman's Real Life Issues Series

Self-help books offering information and advice on a range of key issues. Each book defines the issue and offers ways of understanding and coping with it. The following titles may be relevant and are available from Trotman Publishing (0870 900 2665):

Addictions, Stephen Briggs (2005)

Confidence and Self-Esteem, Nicki Household (2004)

Coping with Life, Jonathan Bradley (2005)

Eating Disorders, Heather Warner (2004)

Family Break-ups, Adele Cherreson Cole (2006)

Stress, Rozina Breen (2004)

Addictions

An addiction is often a cover-up for a deeper problem. Drugs, alcohol, gambling or even the internet can all seem to offer a way of escaping from problems. But, ultimately, they can become *the* problem and only increase your misery. This book provides the background knowledge you need to understand how and why people become addicted, and offers advice and suggestions on who to turn to if you need help coping with this difficult issue.

Confidence & Self-Esteem

Some people ooze confidence while others hide in the kitchen at parties. But being confident isn't about being the loudest, coolest or most sporty – as long as you are happy being *you*, then your confidence soars. If this sounds like a tall order, don't worry – confidence can be learnt and self-esteem can be boosted, and this book is here to show you how…

The *Real Life Issues* are a series of friendly and supportive self-help guides covering the issues that matter to you.

For more information on the series and to buy:
visit www.trotman.co.uk or call 0870 900 2665

www.trotman.co.uk

Coping with Life

Being a teenager is not easy: everything about you and your life is changing. Developing the body and mind of an adult and having to deal with responsibilities such as GCSEs and A levels can leave you reeling. At a time of such intense activity and transformation it is not surprising if you sometimes feel unable to cope. This book offers a set of guidelines for tackling teenage stresses such as relationships with friends, families, sexual identity and plans for the future.

Eating Disorders

Eating disorders can wreck lives and should be nipped in the bud; what may start out as a need to fit in and feel in control can escalate into hospitalisation. An eating disorder is normally a cover-up for another problem that can be tackled through other means such as counselling or therapy. If you are struggling with your attitude to food or know a friend who is, then this book can give you the facts you need to confront the situation.

The *Real Life Issues* are a series of friendly and supportive self-help guides covering the issues that matter to you.

For more information on the series and to buy:
visit www.trotman.co.uk or call 0870 900 2665

www.trotman.co.uk

Family Breakups

The modern family is changing. In fact, if recent trends continue, a quarter of parents will have split up by the time their children are 16 years old. That means there are a lot of you out there experiencing the breakup of your family unit – and it's not an easy thing to deal with. This book provides guidance, coping strategies and reassurance on everything from the legal aspects of divorce to settling in with a new step-family.

Stress

Stress is a condition that we increasingly hear about. It's a by-product of the action-packed, high-expectation lifestyles of the twenty-first century and a small amount of stress is normal and healthy. But if you find yourself stressed out and unable to cope with certain situations, be it exams, a breakup or family tensions, then it could be time to take a step back and seek help. This book can help you work out if you're suffering from stress and provides tips and techniques to help you relax and put things into perspective.

The *Real Life Issues* are a series of friendly and supportive self-help guides covering the issues that matter to you.

For more information on the series and to buy:
visit www.trotman.co.uk or call 0870 900 2665

www.trotman.co.uk